POP CULTURE BIOS

SHAILENE WOODLEY

DIVERGENT'S DARING STAR

HEATHER E. SCHWARTZ

Lerner Publications Company
A division of Lerner Publishing Group, Inc.
241 First Avenue North
Minneapolis, MN 55401 USA

For reading levels and more information, look up this title at
www.lernerbooks.com.

Library of Congress Cataloging-in-Publication Data

Schwartz, Heather E.
    Shailene Woodley : Divergent's daring star / by Heather E.
Schwartz.
       pages   cm — (Pop culture bios)
    Includes index.
    ISBN 978-1-4677-5714-0 (lib. bdg. : alk. paper) —
ISBN 978-1-4677-6097-3 (pbk.) —
ISBN 978-1-4677-6325-7 (eBook)
    1. Woodley, Shailene—Juvenile literature. 2. Actors—United
States—Biography—Juvenile literature. I. Title.
PN2287.W645S35 2015
791.4302'8092—dc23 [B]   2014015915

Manufactured in the United States of America
1 – PC – 12/31/14

INTRODUCTION

Shailene enjoys a red carpet moment at the 2012 Golden Globes.

At the 2012 Golden Globe Awards, Shailene Woodley was practically obligated to show up looking gorgeous. Only a few months before, she'd received exciting news by phone early one morning. Still in her pajamas, she'd learned she'd been nominated for a major award: Best Performance by an Actress in a Supporting Role in a Motion Picture.

It was shocking to think how much her life had changed. *The Descendants* was her first feature film. She'd awed costar George Clooney as well as the movie's director. **The media was already calling her a future star.** And now, she was preparing to walk the red carpet at the Golden Globes—and possibly even win an award.

Shailene arrives at the 2012 Golden Globe Awards in a glamorous white dress.

In her strapless, floor-length dress and heels, Shailene didn't disappoint on arrival. She was called one of the best-dressed starlets at the event. But for the after-party, Shailene changed her clothes. Though she still looked beautiful in a one-shoulder black gown, her shoes grabbed all the attention. No one expected to see toe shoes (a style of running shoes with separated toes) peeping out from underneath her skirt! The media went crazy.

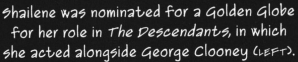

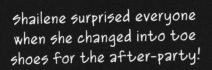

Some critics understood why she'd want to switch from heels to more comfy attire. But the fashion police slammed her choice. Still, no matter what anyone thought or said, Shailene had no regrets. She told the media there were bigger issues to focus on than what she was wearing at a Hollywood event.

Shailene may have made it as a movie star, but she hasn't let that success change her. She is still a girl who doesn't care much for glamour and fame. **She cares more about world issues, the environment, and being true to herself.**

Awards and media attention aside, Shailene is a star who knows who she is and what she thinks is important.

CHAPTER ONE

TOT TO TEEN TALENT

Shailene Woodley makes an appearance at the grand opening of American Girl Place Los Angeles in 2006.

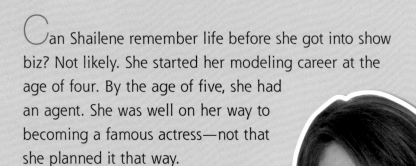

Can Shailene remember life before she got into show biz? Not likely. She started her modeling career at the age of four. By the age of five, she had an agent. She was well on her way to becoming a famous actress—not that she planned it that way.

When Shailene was a kid, acting was just an activity she enjoyed. As she grew up, she still didn't think of it as a career choice. Acting was a way to express herself and her creativity.

BIRTHDAY GIRL

Shailene was born on November 15, 1991, in Simi Valley, California.

Shailene's family includes her father, Lonnie; her mother, Lori; and her younger brother, Tanner.

Some of Shailene's fellow actors from *Replacing Dad* strike a pose. The film's stars included (CLOCKWISE FROM TOP LEFT) Tippi Hedren, Camilla Belle, Erik von Detten, Hayden Tank, and Mary McDonnell.

Playing the Part

Growing up in California, Shailene found acting roles with ease. In 1999, she played the part of Little Girl in *Replacing Dad*, a made-for-TV movie. It was her small-screen debut.

DEBUT =
first public performance

In the years that followed, she made more than sixty commercials and appeared on several hit shows—all while attending public school. Between 2001 and 2007, she was on *Without a Trace, The O.C., Crossing Jordan, Everybody Loves Raymond, My Name is Earl, CSI: NY,* and *Cold Case.* She also made more TV movies. In 2005, she played Felicity in *An American Girl Adventure*—her first lead role.

LEAD =
the biggest role in a show

Shailene was beautiful and talented, with many opportunities to show her stuff as an actress. Life was good. But it was far from perfect.

Shailene as Felicity in An American Girl Adventure

Teen Troubles

When Shailene was in her first year of high school, her parents divorced. Around the same time, she was diagnosed with scoliosis, a curvature of the spine. To correct the problem, she had to wear a plastic back brace from her chest to her hips. It was uncomfortable and made Shailene feel self-conscious.

FIGHTING ON THE HOME FRONT

As a teen, Shailene argued with her mom all the time. She liked to hang out with older kids and didn't want her mother checking up on her. Their relationship improved when Shailene decided to bond with her mom instead of battle.

But Shailene had to wear the brace for more than a year. The only good news: she was allowed to go without it during the hours she worked at her acting jobs.

The way Shailene remembers it, she was awkward as a teen. She felt too skinny and calls herself a late bloomer. But during these years, she landed a plum TV part.

Shailene in her high school yearbook

INDEPENDENT STUDIES

Shailene started studying indigenous cultures on her own time when she was about fifteen years old. Her studies led her to an interest in herbalism—a practice common among many indigenous cultures around the world. Herbalism involves using herbs as medicine.

INDIGENOUS =
original or native

Shailene in 2008 during the
Teen Choice Awards

Budding Star
The Secret Life of the American Teenager was a family drama focused on pregnant teen Amy Juergens. When Shailene won the role of Amy in 2008, she was a junior in high school.

Shailene (THIRD FROM LEFT) poses with the cast of *The Secret Life of the American Teenager.*

She wanted to complete her public school education. Finishing her schooling was going to be a challenge, though. **Shailene's life as an actress was officially in full bloom.**

CHAPTER TWO

PROFESSIONAL BREAKTHROUGH

Shailene (RIGHT) poses for a photo with a friend at a dance during her senior year.

While Shailene was filming her TV series, her teachers and principal pulled together to help her stay in public school. A generous teacher came to Shailene's house each week. In between visits, Shailene did homework in her trailer on the *Secret Life* set.

She kept up and managed to maintain a mostly normal life. For a while, she held onto her job at a paint-your-own pottery studio in Simi Valley. She even went to the prom. In 2009, she graduated from Simi Valley High School.

Shailene grew up in Simi Valley, south of Los Angeles, California. Homes there are nestled between mountains.

In 2010, Shailene and her mother cofounded an organization called All It Takes. This nonprofit group educates young people about healthful eating, environmental issues, and social issues such as bullying.

Shailene gives her mom a hug.

On to New York

When Shailene was eighteen, *Secret Life* went on hiatus. Instead of living large like a famous actress, she took another shot at normal life. She moved to New York City with her boyfriend and applied for jobs at grocery stores and clothing stores. When a job at American Apparel became available, she snapped it up. She loved folding clothes and selling hoodies.

HIATUS = a break

But the relationship with her boyfriend wasn't meant to last. And neither was the job. Within two days, Shailene's agent called her back to California. **A major director wanted to meet with her. How could she say no?**

Alexander Payne, Shailene, and George Clooney arrive on the red carpet for the opening night of *The Descendants* in Beverly Hills, California.

Shailene told her new boss she was sick and hopped a plane home. Just a few months later, she quit American Apparel to star in her first feature film, *The Descendants*. Her costars included one of Hollywood's best-known actors: George Clooney. She would play Alexandra King, the daughter of Clooney's character.

Shailene plays Alexandra in *The Descendants*. Here she shoots a restaurant scene with costar Nick Krause as Sid.

Some of Shailene's fave films include *Rent*, *Dirty Dancing*, *Moulin Rouge!*, and *Pirates of the Caribbean: The Curse of the Black Pearl* (RIGHT).

Hello, Hawaii

In her work on *The Descendants*, Shailene really went the extra mile. Before she started filming, she closely read the book on which the movie was based. She also went hiking and kayaking in Hawaii, where the film is set, to get a feel for the state and its landscape.

Shailene loved exploring Hawaii. In fact, it quickly became her favorite place in the world! But she didn't spend much time researching her character. Shailene wanted to play the part of Alexandra King in a spontaneous and true-to-life way.

Impressive Performance

Shailene's performance earned rave reviews—from the director of the movie, the author of the novel, and many movie critics. Shailene won several awards, including the MTV Movie Award for Breakthrough Performance, and she was nominated for a Golden Globe Award.

All the attention was thrilling. But Shailene felt pressure too. What if she wasn't so good in her next film? What would people say then?

For a while, she considered giving up acting altogether. But then she remembered she didn't do it for her audience. She didn't do it to be famous. **She just loved acting.** She called it her art.

FRESH FACE

Shailene makes a point of going makeup-free at many red carpet events. Since she doesn't wear makeup normally, she doesn't want to project a fake image.

Shailene accepts her 2012 MTV Movie Award for Breakthrough Performance.

CHAPTER THREE

GROUNDED GIRL

Shailene signs autographs for fans in Nashville, Tennessee.

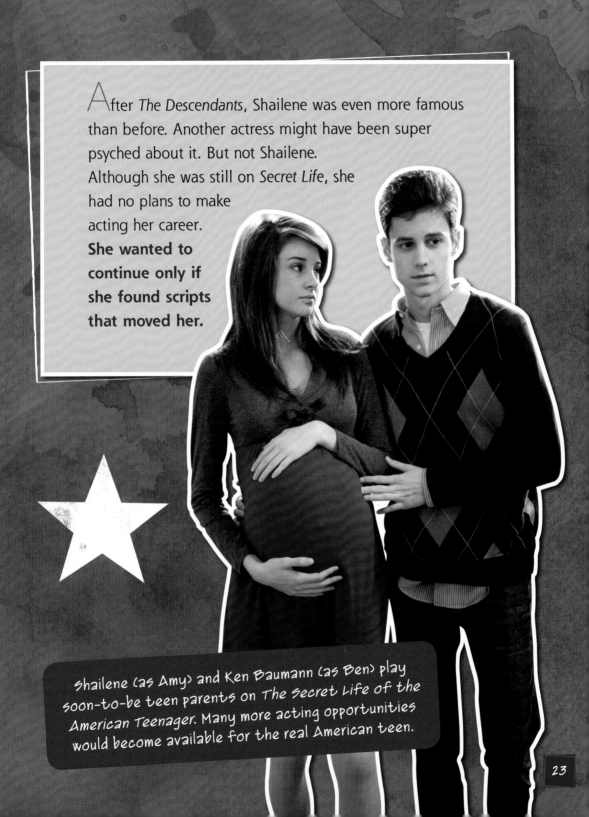

After *The Descendants*, Shailene was even more famous than before. Another actress might have been super psyched about it. But not Shailene. Although she was still on *Secret Life*, she had no plans to make acting her career. **She wanted to continue only if she found scripts that moved her.**

Shailene (as Amy) and Ken Baumann (as Ben) play soon-to-be teen parents on *The Secret Life of the American Teenager*. Many more acting opportunities would become available for the real American teen.

It just so happened that she did. In 2013, *Secret Life* was canceled. But Shailene was asked to audition for a couple of films with story lines she found extremely touching. The first was *The Spectacular Now*, a 2013 movie about an unlikely teenage couple. The second was *White Bird in a Blizzard*, a 2014 movie that tells the story of a girl whose mother disappears. **Shailene got starring roles in both!**

With three films to her name, Shailene was major news all over Hollywood. In fact, she didn't even have to audition for her next gig—which was to be her biggest role yet. The director of the movie *Divergent* wanted Shailene—and only Shailene—to play the lead.

Shailene wasn't sure about committing to a series of films when she won her *Divergent* role. Actress Jennifer Lawrence (RIGHT) helped convince her with an encouraging e-mail.

Divergent's Daredevil

Playing Tris in *Divergent* took more than acting talent. Shailene also had to prove herself as a true survivor. She tapped into her fearless nature and threw herself into the role of a girl the government wants to control—but can't.

Shailene (SEATED) had her first shot at an action movie in *Divergent*.

25

While filming *Divergent* in Chicago, Shailene (ON RIGHT) took an urban survival course. She learned skills like picking locks and jump-starting cars.

For five and a half months, Shailene worked nonstop. She filmed scenes in below-freezing temperatures. She learned to throw knives, shoot guns, and play with fire. She even scaled a 150-foot (46-meter) Ferris wheel—earning respect from the film crew for her courageous attitude.

Filming *Divergent* was extremely challenging for Shailene. But that didn't mean she'd be backing down anytime soon. There were three more movies in the *Divergent* series. That meant three more chances to play Tris. And three more chances to learn and perform new daredevil stunts.

Moving Forward

In 2014, Shailene took on a different kind of challenge. In the movie *The Fault in Our Stars*, she played Hazel Grace Lancaster, a teenager with cancer. It was a big switch from an action film. And it gave her the chance to show she was right for more than one role.

In 2015, she'll star in *Insurgent*, the second film of the *Divergent* series. And in 2016 and 2017, she'll reprise her role in two final films: *Allegiant: Part 1* and *Allegiant: Part 2*. But Shailene has other plans—and dreams—for her future too. Someday she'd like to run an organic farm and produce affordable food for low-income families. She'd like to go to college as well.

For now, Shailene is learning by living—as an actress, an environmentalist, and a young woman who knows her own values. This star is one all-around grounded girl.

REPRISE = to play a character again in a new movie

SUSTAINABLE STYLE

Shailene loves shopping at thrift stores and vintage stores. She says most of her clothes are recycled.

SHAILENE PICS!

Shailene attends the premiere of *The Spectacular Now* in Los Angeles in 2013.

Shailene at a screening of
The Fault in Our Stars

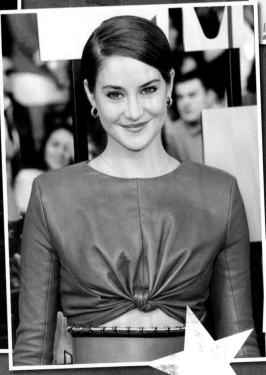

Shailene and her *Fault in Our
Stars* costar Ansel Elgort

Braun, Eric. *John Green: Star Author, Vlogbrother, and Nerdfighter*. Minneapolis: Lerner Publications, 2015. Fans of *The Fault in Our Stars* and Shailene's character in the movie, Hazel Grace, won't want to miss this tell-all bio of the author whose book inspired the film.

Official *Divergent* Movie Site
http://divergentthemovie.com
Visit the official *Divergent* site to get info on the film, see a *Divergent* photo gallery, take a test to see which *Divergent* faction fits you best, and more.

Official *The Fault in Our Stars* Movie Site
http://thefaultinourstarsmovie.com/?gclid=COnVgYrizr4CFepAMgod2CQAkw
Visit this site to see this movie's photos, read about the movie, and submit original movie fan art.

Shailene Woodley on Internet Movie Database
http://www.imdb.com/name/nm0940362
Check out Shailene's IMDb site to learn more about the star.

Shailene Woodley on Twitter
https://twitter.com/shailenewoodley
Follow Shailene on Twitter to learn her thoughts on life.

INDEX

PHOTO ACKNOWLEDGMENTS

The images in this book are used with the permission of: © Jon Kopaloff/FilmMagic/Getty Images, p. 2, 4 (top left); © Frazer Harrison/Getty Images, p. 3 (top), 8 (bottom left); © Kevin Winter/Getty Images, p. 3 (bottom), 21; © s_buckley/Shutterstock.com, p. 4 (top right), 25 (top); © Jeff Vespa/WireImage/Getty Images, p. 4 (bottom left); © Vera Anderson/WireImage/Getty Images, p. 4 (bottom right); © Jason Merritt/Getty Images, p. 5, 29 (bottom left); © Ad Hominem Enterprises/Kobal Collection/Art Resource, p. 6 (top); © Kevork Djansezian/Getty Images, p. 6 (bottom); AP Photo/Ian West/Press Association , p. 7; © Michael Bezjian/WireImage/Getty Images, p. 8 (top left); Byron Purvis/AdMedia/Newscom, p. 8 (right); Katherine Christine/Wenn/Newscom, p. 9; © Larry A. Thompson Productions /Courtesy Everett Collection, p. 10; © Warner Bros./Courtesy Everett Collection, p. 11; Reuters/Fred Prouser/Newscom, p. 12; Seth Poppel Yearbook Library, p. 13, 16 (bottom); Graylock/ABACAUSA.COM/Newscom, p. 14; © AF Archive/Alamy, p. 15, 19 (bottom), 24; © Steve Granitz/WireImage/Getty Images, p. 16 (top right); Byron Purvis/AdMedia/Newscom, p. 16 (top left); © trekandshoot/Alamy, p. 17; © Jason Kempin/Getty Images, p. 18; © Alberto E. Rodriguez/Getty Images, p. 19 (top); © Photos 12/Alamy, p. 20; © Rick Diamond/Allied/Getty Images, p. 22 (bottom); © C Flanigan/FilmMagic/Getty Images, p. 22 (top); The Kobal Collection/ABC-TV/Holmes, Randy, p. 23; © Pictoral Press Limited/Alamy, p. 25 (bottom), 26; AP Photo/20th Century Fox/James Bridges, p. 27; © Globe-Photos/ImageCollect, p. 28 (right); © Jamie McCarthy/Getty Images, p. 28 (top left); © Slaven Vlasic/Getty Images, p. 28 (bottom left); AP Photo/Matt Sayles/Invision for Buzzfeed, p. 29 (top left); © AdMedia/ImageCollect, p. 29 (top right); © Taylor Hill/FilmMagic/Getty Images, p. 29 (bottom right);

Front cover: © Rick Diamond/Getty Images, (small image); © DVS iPhoto Inc./Newscom, (large image). Back cover: © Slaven Vlasic/Getty Images.

Main body text set in Shannon Std Book 12/18.
Typeface provided by Monotype Typography.